iOS 7 User Manual

The Ultimate Guide for iphone and ipad.

Disclaimer

What You Will Find Here

Here's some good news for all iOS users. iOS 7 is finally here and is set to take the world by storm. Well, if you've upgraded to the latest iOS version, there are chances your device would look alien. Interestingly, this latest offering from Apple has a number of amazing features but you may not find them on day one. This can be a little depressing for some of you, but, there's nothing to worry about. *iOS 7 **Starter Guide*** is packed with some useful tips and information to help you browse through the new operating system. So what are you waiting for? Continue reading to find out more about this incredible software.

Table of Contents

Introduction – New Look for iOS 7

The compelling new design of iOS 7 has definitely transformed Apple's mobile operating system interface. If this is the first time you've used an Apple product, there's nothing to worry about. iOS 7 is the seventh and perhaps the most awaited version of Apple's mobile OS. It was unveiled on September 18, 2013 and follows iOS 6.

(Image Courtesy: www.apple.com)

There's not much time for a history lesson, but those of you you've been using iOS 6 know that the sixth version of Apple's mobile OS was overshadowed by controversies. iOS 6 users reported several bugs and not many of them were pleased by the licensing conflicts which seemed to be never ending.

Now fast forward to 2013, iOS 7 is rated as the most obvious change to iOS after the launch of iPhone. Its design is noticeably different from versions launched before it and the icons of iOS 7 use the same colors as the original Apple logo.

Image Courtesy: Wikipedia – Apple_Inc. #Logo

The Home Screen has a totally different appearance and a simple swipe upwards reveals the Control Center.

(Image Courtesy: www.apple.com)

Simple Interface Couldn't Get Any Better!

There's a famous saying that "Simplicity is the Ultimate Sophistication" and now, your iPhone and iPad will not have icons with annoying effects or strange looks. iOS 7 has flat icons with pastel color scheme that gives it an amazing look.

Not to forget, the latest zooming animations look elegant and you would feel excited as you open and close apps.

What's even more incredible about iOS 7 is the fact that as you move your phone or tablet, your wallpaper would start "moving away from your Home icons.

Some of you might need some time to get used to this feature but this feature would surely encourage you to keep looking at your iPhone and iPad.

Image Courtesy: www.apple.com

This shifting of the wallpaper is also known as the "Parallax Effect."

If you've recently updated to iOS 7 and feel dizzy after looking at your device's screen, there's nothing to worry about. Here's a simple trick to disable this parallax effect.

Go to Settings > General > Accessibility and turn Reduced Motion On.

There's no fancy design and the visuals look crisp and clean. Sadly, you don't have much to play with when it comes to customization or themes. Your passcode and dialing screen take the color of your background, but even this looks delightful. The best thing about iOS 7 design is that it feels smooth and the transition between screens is quite elegant. Simply put, iOS 7 is a lot more than a pretty face and here's how you can get iOS 7 on your favorite Apple device.

How You Can Get iOS 7

System Requirements

iOS 7 is compatible with:

1. iPhone 4 and later, i.e. iPhone 4, iPhone 4S, iPhone 5, iPhone 5c, iPhone 5s

2. iPad 2 and later

3. iPad mini

4. iPod touch (5th generation)

This latest offering from Apple supports a number of different languages including English, French, Spanish, Italian and Arabic.

Once you've decided that your iPad or iPhone can run iOS 7, it's time to install the new operating system.

Make sure your device (iPad or iPhone) is connected to a Wi-Fi network. Also, connect your device to a power source. It's always a good idea to back up your data before an update to prevent loss of information.

After you've checked everything, unlock your iPad, go to Settings > General > Software Update. (Note: This feature is only available in devices running iOS 5 or iOS 6.)

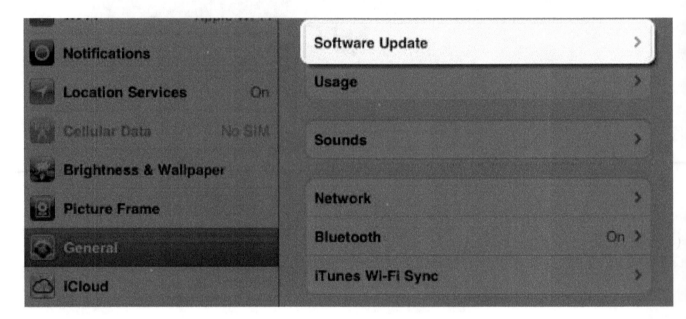

Your iPad should now automatically check for software updates that are available.

You can tap Download to start downloading the update.

Once download is complete, tap install to update your mobile operating system.

If you leave your update to download in the background, you will receive that prompts you to install the update.

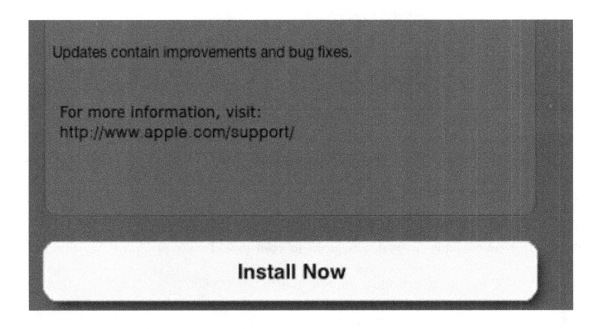

Image Courtesy: www.apple.com

In addition to this method, you can also update your iPad over iTunes.

I Don't Have Enough Space to Install Updates

If you face "space" issues, update your device using iTunes instead of a Wi-Fi connection. You can also retry to download updates after "freeing space" i.e. remove photos, videos, movies and apps you no longer need.

iOS 7 Activation Lock – Save Your iPhone When It Gets Lost!

If you ever lose your favorite gadget, iOS 7's Activation Lock can protect your device from nasty intruders and thieves.

Interestingly, if you decide to delete your device from Apple's Find My iPhone, iOS 7 not only erases your personal data, but the person who finds your iPhone needs to enter your valid Apple ID and password to unlock the device. This means if Activation Lock is in action, the nasty intruder could only use your iPhone as a paperweight!

If all this still sounds alien to you, you need to read this. To set up "Find My iPhone" and "Activation Lock", you need to go to Settings and then tap iCloud.

Scroll down the list until you see "Find My iPhone." Now move the slider so that it shows "On." Your slider now should be on the right side and more importantly, green in color.

If you're iPhone or iPad goes missing, first go to iCloud.com on your computer and enter your valid Apple ID and password.

Once you log in successfully, select **Find My iPhone,** go to **Devices** and then select your device.

Apple's Find My iPhone feature will now track down your device's location. You will be given an option to play a sound or put a message on the lock screen that says "I'm Lost." This message also protects your iPhone with a PIN.

You can also decide to erase your device information completely, which puts your iPhone in Activation Lock mode.

Images Courtesy: www.apple.com

Have a Look at what iOS 7 has In Store

The good thing about Apple's iOS 7 is that it gets a complete design makeover. All of iOS 7 features are amazing, but here are some that do an awesome job.

 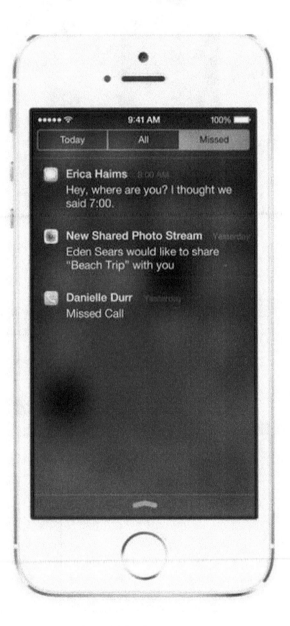

What's your day like?   See what you missed.

Image Courtesy: www.apple.com

Dynamic Text

Now, you have the chance to control the relative size of text in iPhone and iPad applications. Apple's Dynamic Text helps you make text bigger or smaller by moving the slider. All you have to do is set your preference one and all apps that support Dynamic Text will automatically adopt the settings. You can access Dynamic Text from Settings > General > Text Size.

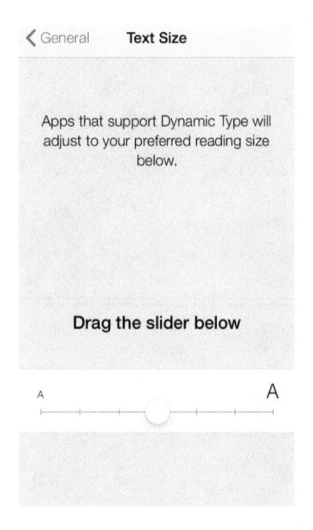

If you want to use text size that's larger than what the Text Size tool allows, use Larger Dynamic Type. For this, first open the Settings App, tap General and then tap Accessibility. Now look for Larger Type and hit your finger on the screen. Enable Larger Dynamic Type and this should be good to go. Now you can set even larger text sizes.

Remember Where I Go!

Hidden inside Location Services, Frequent Locations is another interesting iOS 7 feature. When enabled, this feature allows your iPhone to remember all places you've visited. You can turn on Frequent Locations under Settings > Privacy > Location Services > System Services. Overall, this iPhone feature is an easy way to remember all places you've been recently.

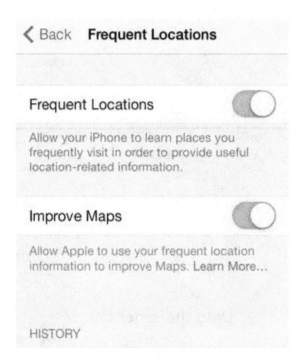

Better Control Center

One of most interesting features to come to iOS 7 is the "One Swipe" Control Center. Finally you don't have to tap multiple icons to get a single task done and this will definitely help you save time.

What's really amazing about the Control Center is the fact that it is available from any screen. Let's say you have to switch on your Wi-Fi. All you need to do is swipe up from the bottom of your display screen and tap the Wi-Fi icon.

Image Courtesy: www.apple.com

This action also gives quick access to handy tools such as Bluetooth, screen brightness control, screen rotation, Airplane mode as well as music controls. This is not all. You can also set an alarm and open the camera or calculator using the "One Swipe" action. Not to forget, you can connect to AirPlay devices and switch on your flashlight.

A Personalized Notification Center

If you have a look at the Notifications pull-down menu, you will find three tabs "Today", "All" and "Missed." All and Missed show your alerts and all calls and messages you've missed respectively. And the special "today" pane keeps track of all tasks you have scheduled for the day, i.e. today.

Image Courtesy: www.apple.com

This was a small and useful explanation of the notifications pull-down menu. Interestingly, many iOS 7 users find the notification menu to be quite annoying especially when it takes up lots of space.

If you hate to scroll down everything and don't want to read every notification that pops up, there's nothing to worry about. Customizing your notification center is not a big deal and here's how you can control the notifications that appear on your iPhone screen. You can also use these customization tricks if you prefer "open space" or a notification menu where notifications are not jammed into one screen.

How You Can Customize Your Notification Center

By default, the Today view in iOS 7 provides you with the much needed information about

1. Weather forecast

2. Your calendar

3. Reminders

4. To-do-list

5. Stock quotes

6. Calendar events for tomorrow

Maybe you're not really interested in stocks or you want to tweak what appears in the Today view. To change the way your Today view is displayed, go to Settings app, select Notification

Center settings and then scroll down the list until you find the Today View heading. Now you can decide what should appear on your Today screen with the help of few toggles.

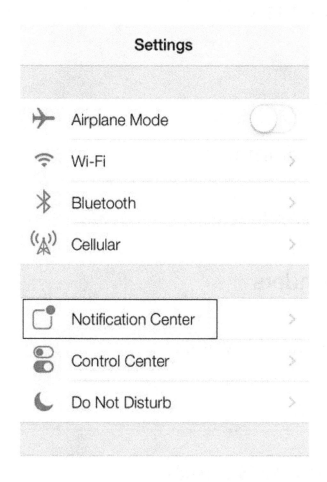

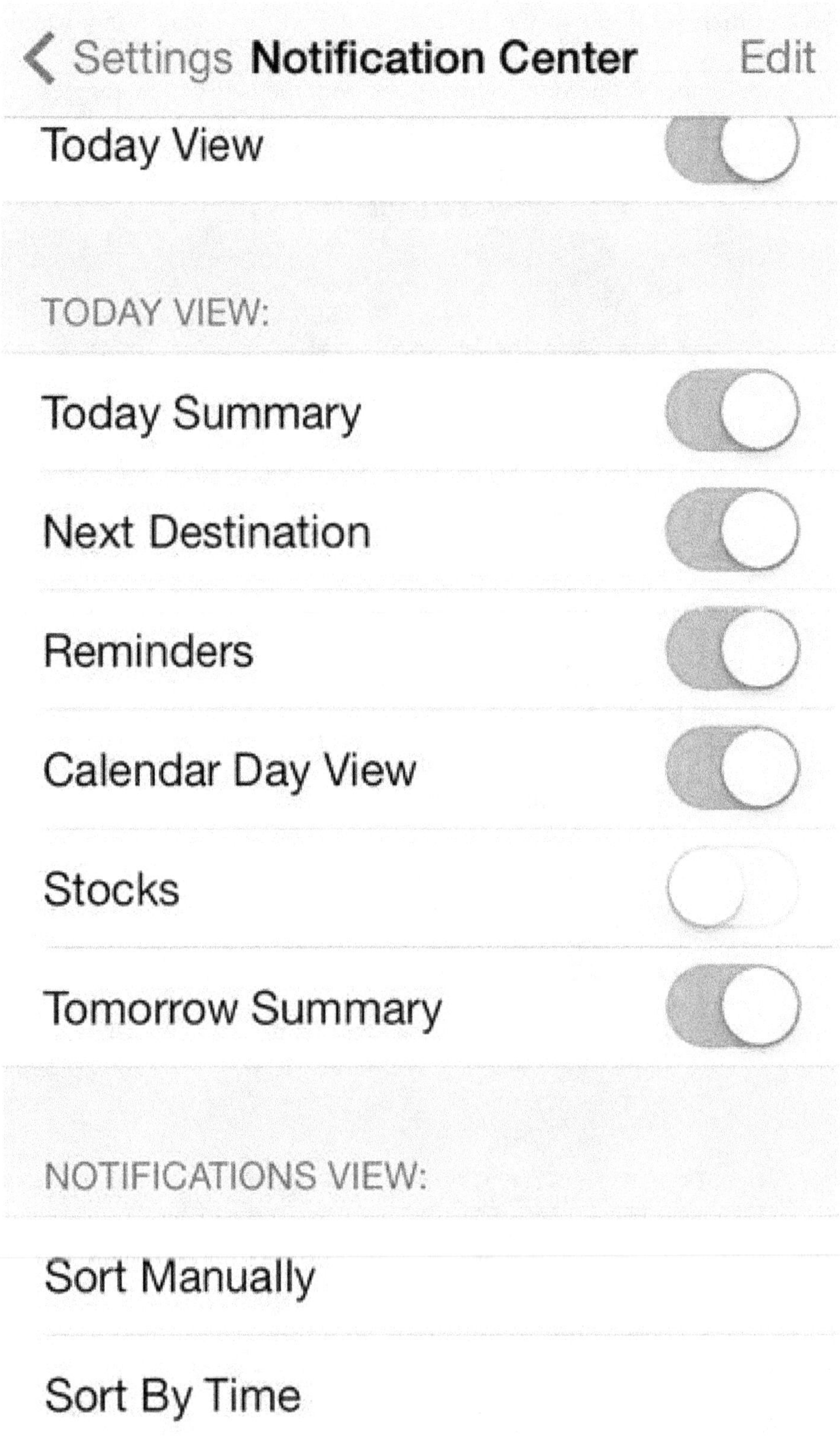

‹ Settings Notification Center   Edit

Today View

TODAY VIEW:

Today Summary

Next Destination

Reminders

Calendar Day View

Stocks

Tomorrow Summary

NOTIFICATIONS VIEW:

Sort Manually

Sort By Time

Wrong numbers might keep bothering you and there's nothing you can do about it. Well, now iOS 7 gives you the chance to block those nasty callers and you could do it quite easily.

To block someone already on your iPhone contact list, open the **Contacts** app and select the desired contact. Scroll down the list of options and then select **Block this Caller**.

Send Message

Share Contact

Add to Favorites

Block this Caller

☆ Favorites   🕐 Recents   🎧 Contacts   ⠿ Keypad   ◯◯ Voicemail

To edit your blocked contact list, first go to the Settings app and then select **Phone, Messages, or FaceTime settings**.

Scroll down the screen until you see "Blocked." You can then edit, i.e. add or remove people from your list.

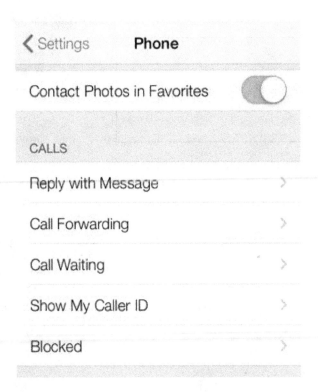

To add a contact to your Blocked list, tap "Add New." Similarly, swipe a contact's name from right to left and then tap the **Unblock** button that appears on your screen to remove the contact from your Blocked list.

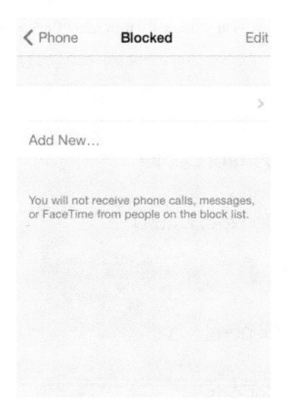

Remember, all blocked contacts won't be able to call you or send a text message. Plus, blocking a contact means you can no longer have a FaceTime conversation with them. Another thing you need to keep in mind is that you cannot block text messages from a sender if you've allowed them to call you.

Do Not Disturb – That's Better!

Now with iOS 7, you can decide whether or not you want to entertain phone calls from your contacts. If you don't want to be disturbed, you can block phone calls from every contact. To change your DND preferences, go to Settings and then select Do Not Disturb.

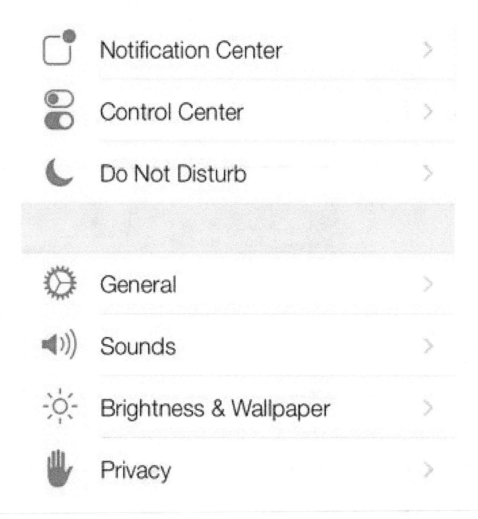

Allow Calls From   No One >

Incoming calls or messages from everyone will be silenced.

Repeated Calls

When enabled, a second call from the same person within three minutes will not be silenced.

SILENCE:

Always

Only while iPhone is locked

SILENCE:

Always

Only while iPhone is locked

Incoming calls and notifications will be silenced while iPhone is either locked or unlocked.

SILENCE:

Always

Only while iPhone is locked ✓

Incoming calls and notifications will be
silenced while iPhone is locked.

The most amazing thing about iOS 7 is that it allows you to block all calls except those you want. You can choose Favorites or specific contact groups listed on your iPhone under "Allow Call From" and get the incoming calls and notifications.

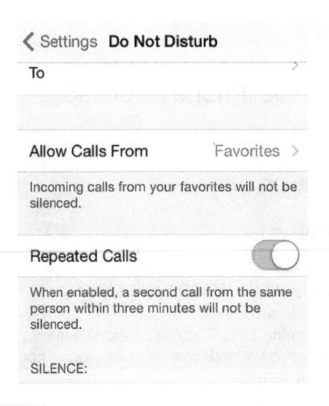

Turn On Automatic App Updates

Interestingly, you'll love iOS 7 even more because it has a hidden feature that allows your iPhone and iPad to download and install app updates automatically. This means your installed apps will be upgraded as soon as app updates become available.

To enable automatic updates for your device, first open the Settings app and then select iTunes and App Store. Toggle the settings **On and Off** so that they suit your preference.

For your safety, iOS 7 downloads and installs automatic updates only when a Wi-Fi connection is available. You can turn on updates via Cellular Data, but you have to be careful especially if you have a limited or expensive data plan.

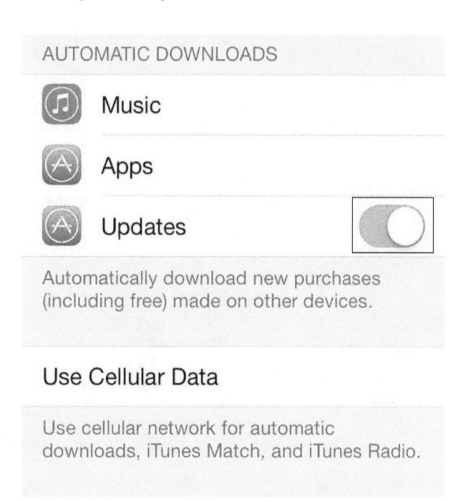

Also, you cannot prevent iOS 7 from installing new updates once you've enabled it. For example, if you are not really interested in the newer version of any app, there's no way you can avoid the update. The only thing you can do is turn off automatic updates completely if you fear that newer updates would be horrible.

Simply put, Automatic Update feature is a lifesaver if you have lots of apps or you hate looking at the updates notifications. On the other hand, it can become a nightmare if the updated version is simply awful.

Unfortunately, you have no middle ground here, the feature can only be always on or always off.

Multitasking – The Best Way to Switch between Apps

Multitasking has become a hot topic these days and iOS 7 ensures that you become a multitasking expert. Now, you can get a clear preview of your open apps when you double tap the Home button. And, being able to quit the apps without going into individual windows is exactly what you need especially when you're short of time. You can swipe left or right to find the app you want or simply swipe up on the preview image to close the app.

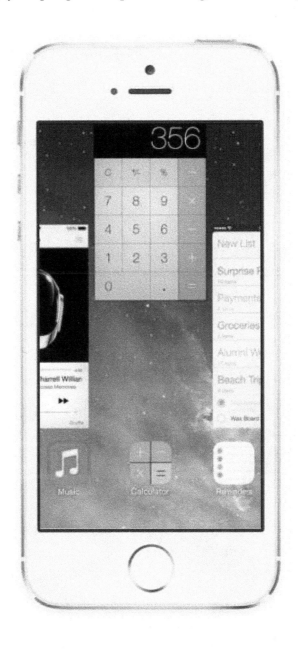

If you want to start working on a different app, simply double tap the Home button, tap the desired preview image and you'll automatically go to the selected app.

Background App Refresh

You can control the way apps "refresh" when they're not running. If you turn on Background App Refresh under Settings > General > Background App Refresh, your app content will be refreshed automatically and you don't have to waste time for update when the application is launched. You can change this option anytime you want.

Another great thing about App Refresh is the fact that iOS 7 gives you (the device owner) the chance to enable or disable App Refresh on app-by-app basis.

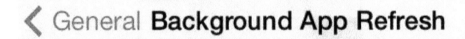

Allow apps to refresh their content when on Wi-Fi or cellular, or use Location Services, in the background. Turning off apps may help preserve battery life.

Do Everything New While Surfing Safari

The Safari browser for iPhone and iPad has also undergone lots of changes to make your iOS 7 browsing experience even better. But, at its core usability, Safari looks similar to its predecessors. Interestingly, Apple wanted to renovate Safari completely so that it can compete with the increasingly popular third party web browsers.

The moment you launch Safari, you'll find everything with a visual redesign. The first thing you'll notice is the incredible "full screen" look, where the search field (search box at the top of your screen) and the navigation buttons (toolbar at the bottom of your screen) disappear while you're busy browsing.

Image Courtesy: www.apple.com

The Unified "Smart Box"

The earlier versions of Safari had two separate boxes, i.e. search box on the left and the address box on the right.

Safari in iOS 7 has merged both boxes and you'll only find one "multi-purpose" box.

You have much more flexibility with browser windows as well. Now, instead of swiping left and right to check out all what you've opened, you can simply preview all your windows stacked as vertical scrolling cards.

Not many iPhone and iPad users are happy with this feature because it's something that has been on Android phones for a longer time.

The good news is that you are not limited to 2 or 3 windows. With iOS 7, you can open up to 7 or 8 windows and simply swipe the selected window to the left side to close it as with Android. You can also use the tiny cross sign on the left side of the window to close it.

You can use gestures to navigate back and forth or browse through your Safari history. The previous webpage can be accessed by swiping from the left edge of your screen. Similarly, you can go forward by swiping from the right edge of your iPhone or iPad display screen.

As mentioned earlier, iOS 7 has merged the search and address bar into a new unified smart box. This box allows you to type the URL of the website or search for your desired term. You can access this smart box by tapping your screen or pulling it down from the top.

As you continue typing, iOS 7 will display the related searches and this includes suggestions from Google Search, your Bookmarks, your browsing history and of course suggestions from the search engine you're using.

Safari Keyboard with a Dot

Sadly, Apple has discarded the .com button from the iOS 7 Keyboard and replaced it with a simple dot. This improvement has been made to make more room for the space bar and you can tap and hold the dot to access all major domain extensions.

Browse and Add Favorites

Once you tap on the search field, Safari will display icons for all your favorites, which is a pretty interesting feature. Not only you get a preview of all your favorites, but you can tap the icon for quick and easy access to your favorite websites.

If you want to add a website as a favorite, simply tap on the share button first, and then tap on Bookmarks. You can then add your Bookmarks to the Favorites folder. You also have the option to select which folder should contain your favorites. To change your preferences go to Settings > Safari > Favorites.

Apple has also added much needed parental controls to Safari. If you want to restrict the use of your browser, go to Settings > General > Restrictions > Websites under Allowed Content to make changes.

With Safari parental controls, you can

1. allow kids to visit all websites
2. Limit access to all adult websites automatically.

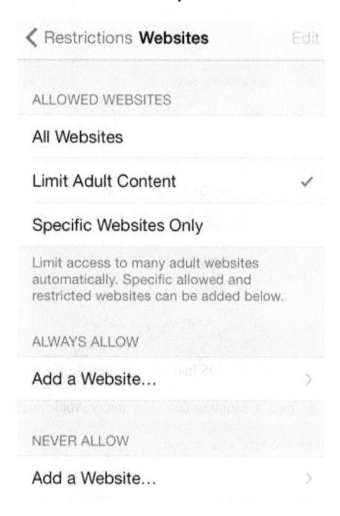

3. Allow access to specific websites only. Apple has also added a list of children friendly websites like Discovery Kids, Disney and National Geographic – Kids which you can use. To add another website, simply tap on "Add a Website" option.

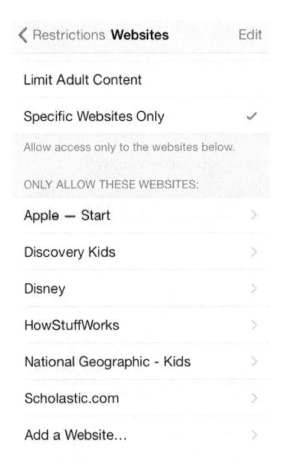

Private Browsing

Interestingly, the earlier versions of iOS had one common problem – private browsing session on Safari was nothing less than a daunting task. Not many Apple users were keen to try Safari's private browsing feature and here's the reason.

If you've used iOS 6, you'll know that starting a private browsing session was a long, tedious process. First, you have to exit your browser and then open Safari preferences to enable Private Browsing.

Your troubles just didn't end here. Safari would then prompt you to answer a question.

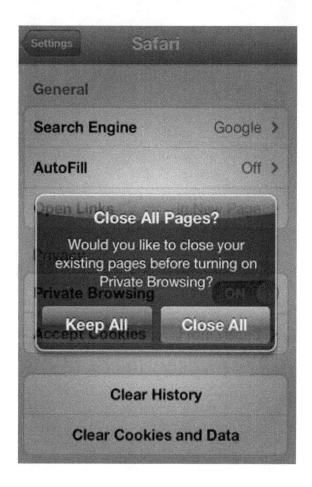

For your ease, Apple has decided to include a "Private browsing" button in the bottom left corner of every new tab you open. So, if you want to start private browsing, simply open a new tab and hit the Private button.

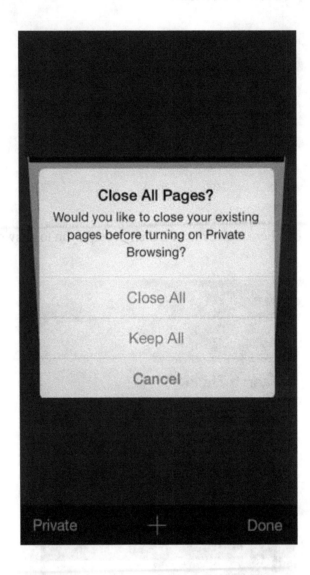

To differentiate between Private and normal browsing modes, Apple has given a darker color scheme to all windows and tabs that are opened in Private mode.

The Bookmarks Tab

iOS 7 has also made a lot of improvements to the bookmarks interface as visible in Safari. Your bookmarks bar i.e. your Favorites are now displayed whenever you open a new tab.

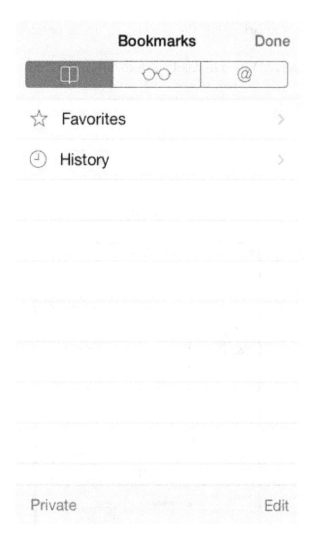

As you can see, the Bookmarks menu has three different tabs, i.e. Bookmarks, Reading List and Shared Links. Shared Links is another exciting feature in iOS 7.

Not only the new Bookmarks menu is a lot cleaner, but you can enter a private browsing session using the links saved within your Bookmarks, Reading List and Shared Links.

Shared Links

With Shared Links, you can see all the URLs in your Twitter timeline as well as who posted them and what people had to say about them.

Basically, this new iOS feature brings all the tweets, i.e. links posted by people you follow on Twitter in one convenient place. You can easily extract all of the desired links posted on Twitter and review them on the internet.

Image Courtesy: www.apple.com

Lots of things you do on the internet require you to enter passwords or personal information. Now with iOS 7 and iCloud, your favorite Apple device can remember your personal info, passwords as well as credit card numbers. And the best part is that Safari will enter the information automatically whenever and wherever you want.

Image Courtesy: www.apple.com

You'll see that Safari for iOS 7 has a new section for saving credit card information. Like other passwords and confidential data, you can view and save your credit card information on your device. Remember, you'll have to enter your valid username and password to retrieve the personal and credit card information you've saved.

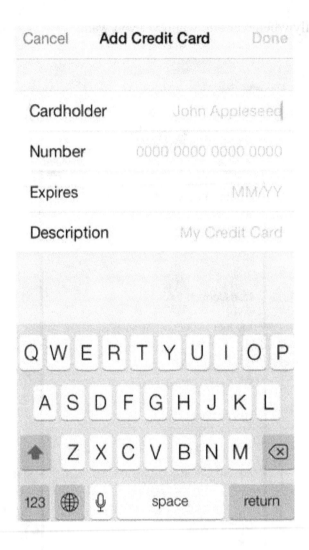

Simply put, it's safe to say that Safari for iOS 7 is much better than its predecessor in nearly every single way you can think of.

iOS 7 and Incredible Camera Features

Let the "Artist" Free

You can now access your iPhone or iPad camera from anywhere in iOS 7 and this is due to the all new Control Center "single swipe." Yes, iOS 7 translucent swipe menu includes a shortcut for the camera app.

Camera in iOS 7 is ideal to unleash the artist within you. You can put your photography skills into action and use all shooting formats – still, video and panorama.

What's even more exciting is that you can snap your photo with a swipe. Yes, it's really simple and quick to capture what you want, more importantly the way you want. And new filters in iOS 7 let you do even more with every snapshot. You can give it a retro feel or spice up the contrast. There's also an option to go black and white. Quite simply, there's no limit to what you can do.

The position of the shutter button, LED flash toggle as well as front-facing/rear facing camera toggle remains the same. The first thing you'll notice after you launch the camera app is that camera modes are listed horizontally. The default mode is Photo. You'll find Square and Pano (panorama) towards the right side of your screen. Video capture mode is on the left side.

Apple has removed the options menu in iOS 7. You can toggle or switch between video and the panorama mode by swiping on the shutter button. As you switch between different modes, you'll see the screen go blur.

iOS 7's Camera has a new mode called Square, a feature that allows you to take square photos. This feature is similar to something you get on Instagram.

Other photo filters can be accessed by tapping the button located on the right of the shutter button. Once you tap on the filters button or tile, you'll see a number of real-time filter effects such as Mono, Tonal, Noir, Fade, Chrome, Process, Transfer and Instant. All you need to do is tap on one of them and then tap the shutter button to fill your photo with the desired effect.

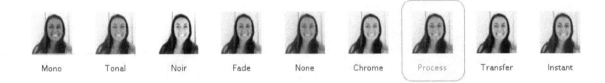

Images Courtesy: www.apple.com

You can apply filters to photos taken in Square and Photo mode, but this feature is not available for videos and panorama mode.

iOS 7 gives you the option to apply these filters on photos in your camera roll. If you want to edit photos in your camera roll, first tap on a photo and then tap on the Edit button. Now select the filter icon and this should add the filter effect to your photo.

The best part is that taking photos in iOS 7 is lightning fast. There's no delay when you tap on the shutter button, which unfortunately was one of the most annoying things about the Camera app in earlier iOS 7. Yes, camera app in iOS 7 is truly instantaneous.

Recording Video

Surprisingly, you don't have to move to zoom in your video while recording on iOS 7. All you have to do is use the familiar pinch-to-zoom gesture when your video is recording.

Try placing two fingers on your device's screen with Video mode selected and then move them apart to zoom in. Bring your fingers back together to zoom out.

One thing you need to keep in mind is that when you zoom, the quality of your video may suffer. You can use the gesture to zoom in and zoom out but don't go overboard or zoom in and out repeatedly while recording your video.

Panorama Shot

iOS 7 allows you to take the panorama shot.

Move iPhone continuously when taking a Panorama.

HDR Option

The HDR option you find on your screen is only available for the Photo and Square mode.

If you're curious to know more about HDR, it is a special technique where 3 photos are taken in rapid succession. HDR photos have one normal, one under-exposed, and one over-exposed photo and all 3 images are then combined together to create an enhanced photo.

Taking Photos in Burst Mode

While taking a photo on iOS 7 camera app, you can hold your onscreen shutter button or the volume-up button as long as you'd want to capture a burst of photos, i.e. successive photos at the impressive rate of 10 frames per second.

Apple has done a lot of work revamping the camera app and the photo app is no different. The latest Photos app is cleaner, neater and more organized. Your photos are placed into albums and organized based on date taken as well as location.

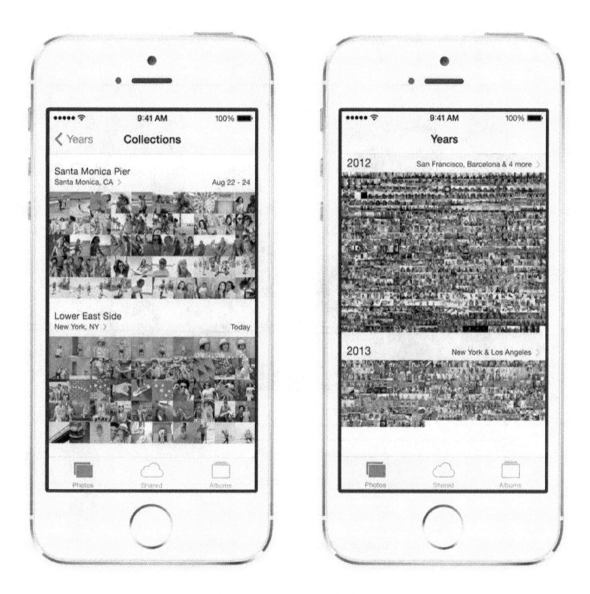

You can see that photos are categorized by year and placed in a dense mosaic. Now, you can touch and hold your screen to zoom into a picture from the multiple images and then drag your finger to preview other photos. This is a simple trick but you can also tap the year and then cut down to dates and locations if you're looking for a specific image.

All your Collections are organized into Moments according to date and location they were taken.

Sharing Photos

Image Courtesy: www.apple.com

To share an image, all you have to do is tap the Share button. You'll notice many of the same sharing features that were available in the previous operating system, but there are a few new ones as well. For example, the new option to create an image slideshow.

Speaking of shared Photo Streams, Apple now refers it as Shared Streams. You can find your shared streams under the Shared tab. You'll also find a new Activity view which as the name suggests, displays any recent activity on shared streams.

Another major improvement over iOS 6 is that you can now collaborate with multiple people when sharing your photos. Let's say you've created and shared an album with your friends. With iOS 7, your friends can add photos of their own rather than just viewing and commenting on the images you've added. Of course, it's up to you to decide whether subscribers (people who can view your shared album) can only view pictures or can add their own images.

Sharing photos on iOS 7 is really easy with iCloud and AirDrop. If you don't want to send images via email or text, try sharing your images with AirDrop for iOS. AirDrop allows you to share photos and videos quickly and easily, more importantly using the Share button.

Simply tap Share and then select the person you want to share the images with. AirDrop does the rest for you with little help from Wi-Fi and Bluetooth.

Siri and iOS 7

Apple's favorite digital assistant also gets a makeover in this operating system revamp.

You'll notice a new sound wave animation at the bottom of your screen as you speak. Siri's results now appear as full screen view, not annoying tiny cards. You'll also feel that Siri in iOS 7 is a little faster to respond to your search queries but Google Search still wins the battle for fastest voice search response time.

62

Images Courtesy: www.apple.com

By far the best and of course the most useful addition to iOS 7 Siri is that Apple's digital assistant can now perform actions. You can use Siri to play a voice mail, turn on Bluetooth, and even adjust your brightness settings. The latest Siri can also search Wikipedia and Twitter.

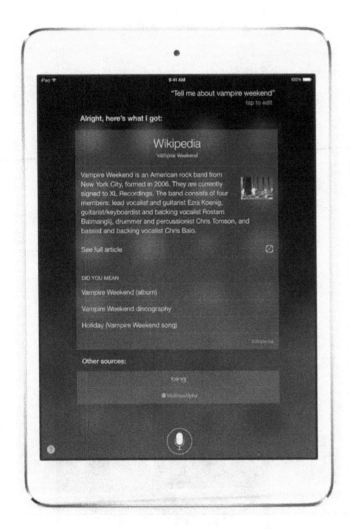 

Image Courtesy: www.apple.com

Siri, Apple's smart virtual assistant now gets a new voice in iOS 7. Yes, your virtual assistant also has some "new voices" and you can have a male assistant if you prefer.

If you want to change Siri's female voice, first open the Settings app and then go to General. Select **Siri** and then tap Voice Gender. There it is. You can now choose a different female voice, interestingly one that sounds a little less robotic and there's a male voice as well. Go for the 2nd option if you want Siri to become a new personality.

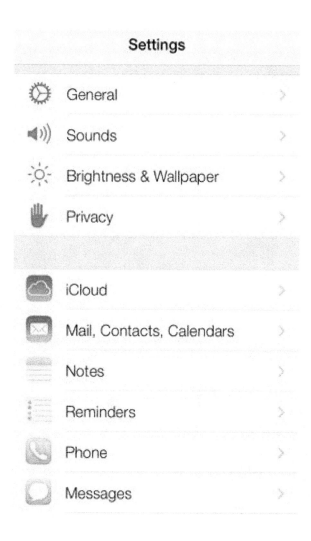

‹ Settings   **General**

| About | › |
| Software Update | › |

Siri	›
Spotlight Search	›
Text Size	›
Accessibility	›

| Usage | › |
| Background App Refresh | › |

‹ General   **Siri**

| Siri | ⬤ |

Siri helps you get things done just by asking. You can make a FaceTime call, send a message, dictate a note, or even find a restaurant. About Siri and Privacy...

Language	›
Voice Gender	Female ›
Voice Feedback	Always ›
My Info	›

To talk to Siri, press and hold the home button and speak.

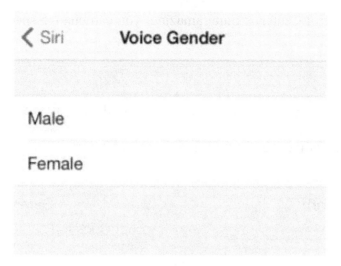

Well, you only have one male and one female voice so your options are not that interesting.

Unfortunately, voice change options are further limited if you're using a language other than US or Canadian English. Sorry other language users, but still some choice is always better than none.

Remember, Siri in iOS 7 is smarter than she was in iOS 6, so now you can make her do things like change your screen's brightness or turn off Bluetooth.

Interestingly, Siri has also become more conversational, and she knows exactly when you'll speak and waits for it. Now you won't be prompted to tap the microphone button again. Once you've made the desired changes, just give it a try. You'll surely be pleased with the changes.

Siri is All Set to Shine – Discover Some Cool Siri Tips

1. Change your device settings

As mentioned earlier, Siri can be used to change settings like Bluetooth, screen brightness and Airplane Mode. When you say "Turn off Bluetooth," Siri is really quick to obey your orders.

Although the new Control Center is quite amazing, you can change specific settings with little help from Siri.

If you want to find a setting, simply ask Siri to take you there. Say something like "change text size" or "change Safari settings" and you'll find the right Settings menu.

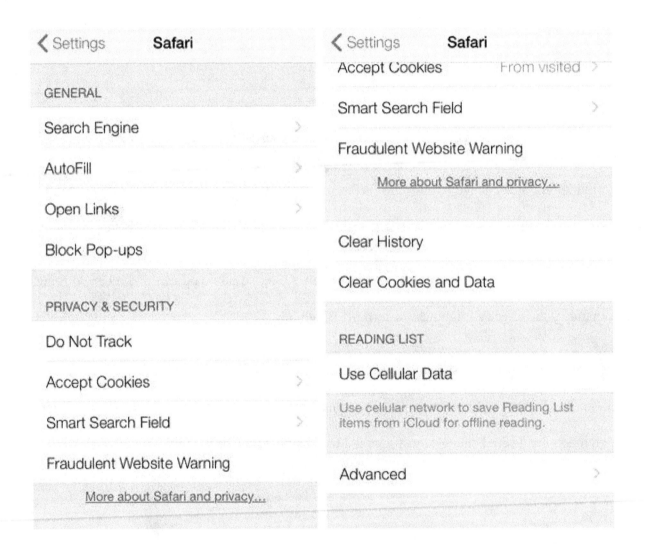

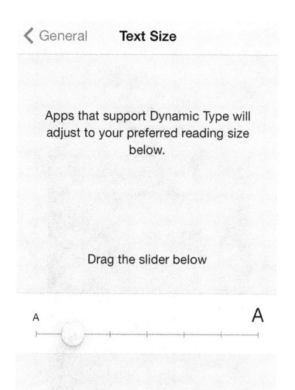

2. Help Siri learn new things

Image Courtesy: www.apple.com

Ok, Siri is giving you troubles and cannot pronounce the name of your best friend or co-worker.

Now, you don't have to get angry, instead train Siri and help her get things right.

All you have to say is "pronounce [person's name]" and then follow the steps that appear on your

screen.

"Learn how to pronounce my name"

tap to edit

OK, how do you pronounce the name   ?

OK, thank you. Which pronunciation should I use?

OK, how do you pronounce the name   ?

OK, thank you. Which pronunciation should I use?

Pronounce

?

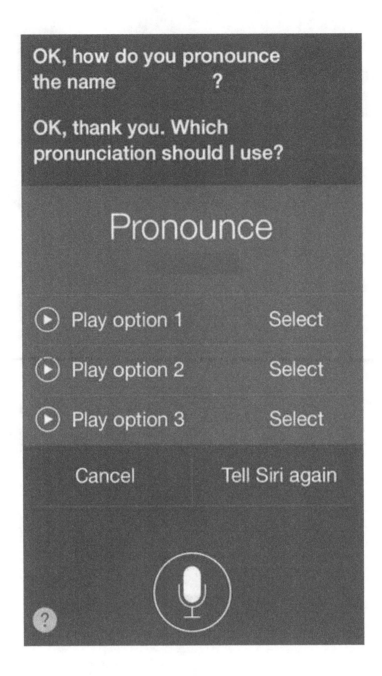

3. Manage your favorite tweets

Siri now has excellent Twitter integration and you'll never miss out on what's trending.

In fact, you can ask Siri things like, "Hey, what's trending on Twitter right now?"

Siri will then Search Twitter for hash tag [your query] and give Twitter based results.

Image Courtesy: www.apple.com

4.   Choose and Set Your Favorite Search Engine

Whether you like it or not, Siri's default search engine is Microsoft's Bing. But, you don't have to be shocked after hearing this.

If you request Siri to "search Google for" or "search Wikipedia for" something, Siri will obey your commands and give you relevant results in Safari, not Siri's own tiny page.

5. Stay Connected with your Emails

Even earlier versions of Siri told you if you had any new emails or messages and new Siri is one step ahead.

Siri in iOS 7 can actually start reading your new messages to you if you say, "Read my email." In addition to your message, you'll hear the sender's name, the date and time of your message, as well as the subject line.

This feature can also be used to checkout messages from one particular sender. You can say something like "read my latest email from my boss" or "Do I have any new emails from my boss?"

To view the full message, simply tap the onscreen preview to open up Mail app. You can also ask Siri to read emails in order, like "Read the second one."

6. Turn off Maps or Navigation

Apple's Maps can get you where you need to go but if you're driving on a familiar route, you can switch off navigation to save battery.

Simply tell Siri to "cancel navigation" and you should be good to go.

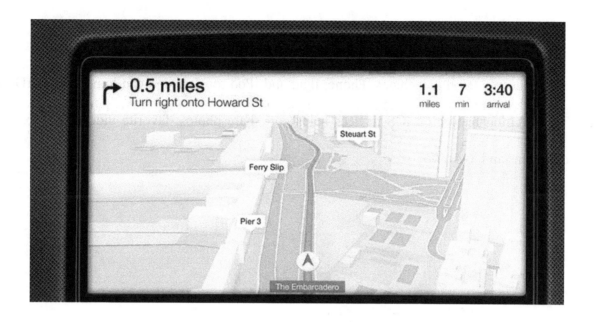

7. Turn on iTunes Radio

Are you in the mood for a little Daft Punk or maybe some other track?

Siri loves to play with the iTunes Radio dial and when you ask for an artist or a specific track, Siri will play it right up.

Just say "Play iTunes Radio Daft Punk" and so on.

Get to Know AirDrop

Now iOS 7 users (and this includes iPhone, iPad and iPod touch users) can join in the AirDrop fun. This exciting feature on iOS devices helps you share photos, favorite videos, web pages, map directions and lots more.

AirDrop. Drop everything.

AirDrop only works over Wi-Fi and Bluetooth, and you cannot make it work over the cellular networks. What's even more interesting is the fact that you don't even have to be on the same Wi-Fi network as your friend's for it to work. AirDrop will automatically create a temporary direct connection with your friend's device as long as you both are within a close proximity.

You also need to understand that AirDrop does not work on all iOS 7 compatible devices.

Yes, this feature only works with iPhone 5 and newer versions, the 4th-generation iPad and iPad Mini and the 5th-generation iPod Touch and later versions. Plus, you also need an iCloud account in order to use AirDrop transfers. All AirDrop transfers are encrypted for your security.

How You Can Share Files Using AirDrop

To start sharing a file, make sure you and the other person have AirDrop turned on. Simply swipe up from the bottom of your screen to open Control Center, and then tap AirDrop.

Image Courtesy: www.apple.com

If you want to receive AirDrop transfers only from people who are in your contacts list, select Contacts Only. To share your files with every person nearby, tap EVERYONE. All you have to do is ask people to turn on AirDrop when you do.

Next, open the files you want to share.

Let's say you want to share your photos.

Open your photo and then locate the share button, the tiny icon that has pointed arrows. When the other person has AirDrop turned on, you should see them along the top of the sharing panel. Select the person you want to share, and they'll get a notification to accept or reject the photo. Once the person taps the *Accept* button, your phone will automatically send the photo to their device.

Image Courtesy: www.apple.com

Image Courtesy: www.apple.com

Want to be Available or Not?

Sadly, you're automatically visible in AirDrop when you turn it on. But with iOS 7, you can

yourself visible to anyone or no one at all.

One tap in one swipe Control Center is all what you need to do.

Image Courtesy: www.apple.com

Other Miscellaneous Features

Wallpapers and Brightness

Apple's iOS 7 also has excellent support for "dynamic" wallpapers, not to forget the all new Brightness & Wallpaper settings you get on your device. There are different sections for "Dynamic" and "Stills" wallpapers and new static wallpapers have also been added. You can see wallpaper previews before you make a final decision.

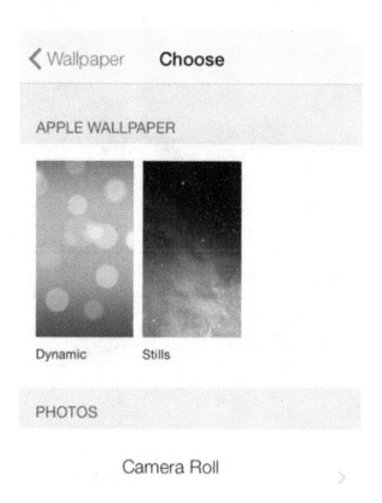

Stay Secure – Privacy Settings

Luckily, iOS 7 now allows you to set privacy controls for every individual app on your device.

And, you can toggle settings for each and every app to suit your preferences.

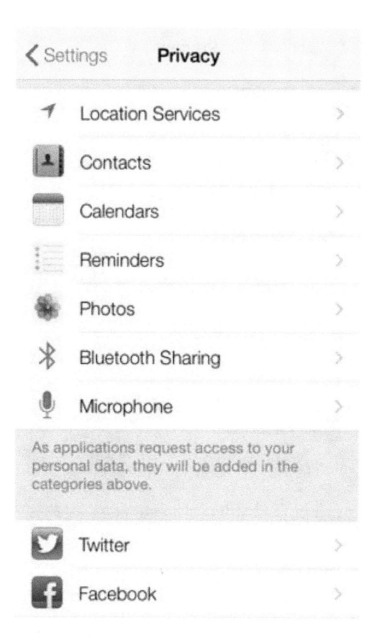

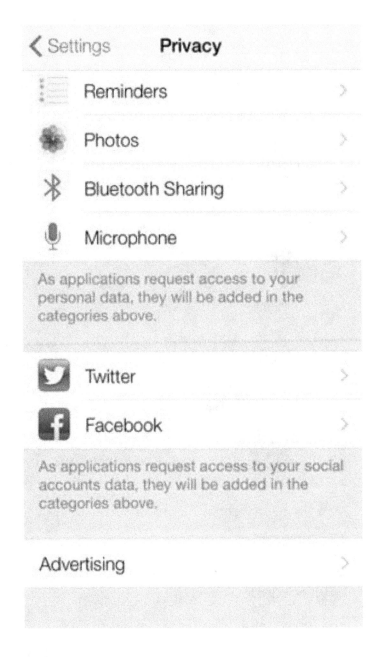

iCloud is the Way to Go

Apple's iCloud is a simple way to put your content across all your devices. Plus, it's really easy to setup iCloud on all Apple devices. That's the way content transfer should be and iOS 7 makes it even better.

If you buy a song from iTunes, you don't have to download it again and again to enjoy it on multiple devices. And the same applies to a word document you just edited on your Mac book. iCloud takes care of everything and your content will automatically be synced across all devices that have iCloud.

If you've just been on a vacation, simply share your photos and videos with iCloud with everyone in your group.

You can also send a location-based alert to your family and they'll know exactly where you are and when you will arrive. Simply put iCloud helps you can share exactly what you want and of course, with the right people.

Image Courtesy: www.apple.com

If you ever lose your device, iCloud can also help you find it. What's even better is that iCloud restricts every unauthorized person from using your device while it is lost.

Remember, all information on your iPhone, iPad and even iPod touch can be backed up with iCloud and you can easily restore and recover it on your new device if you ever need it.

iCloud Keychain

As mentioned earlier, lots of websites especially online shopping require passwords and now you can ask iCloud to remember all your important passwords and credit card numbers. Whenever, you access websites that require passwords, Safari will enter them automatically on all your approved iOS 7 devices.

Mail, Contacts and Calendar

The Mail settings in iOS 7 remain mostly the same as previous versions; however, the much needed support for secondary e-mail addresses has been added.

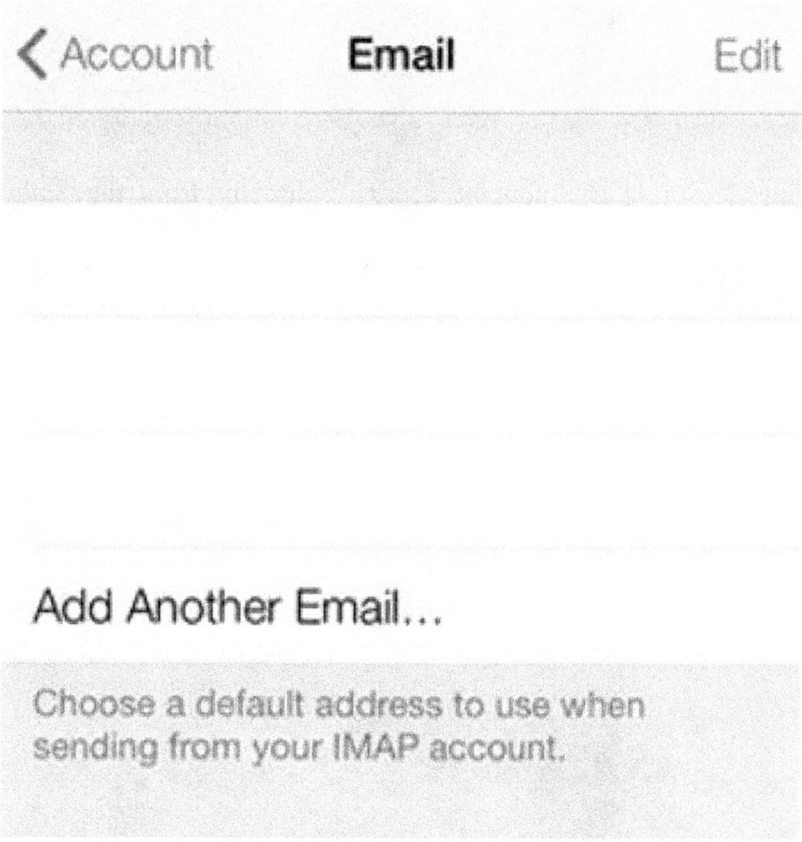

‹ Account   **Email**   Edit

Add Another Email…

Choose a default address to use when sending from your IMAP account.

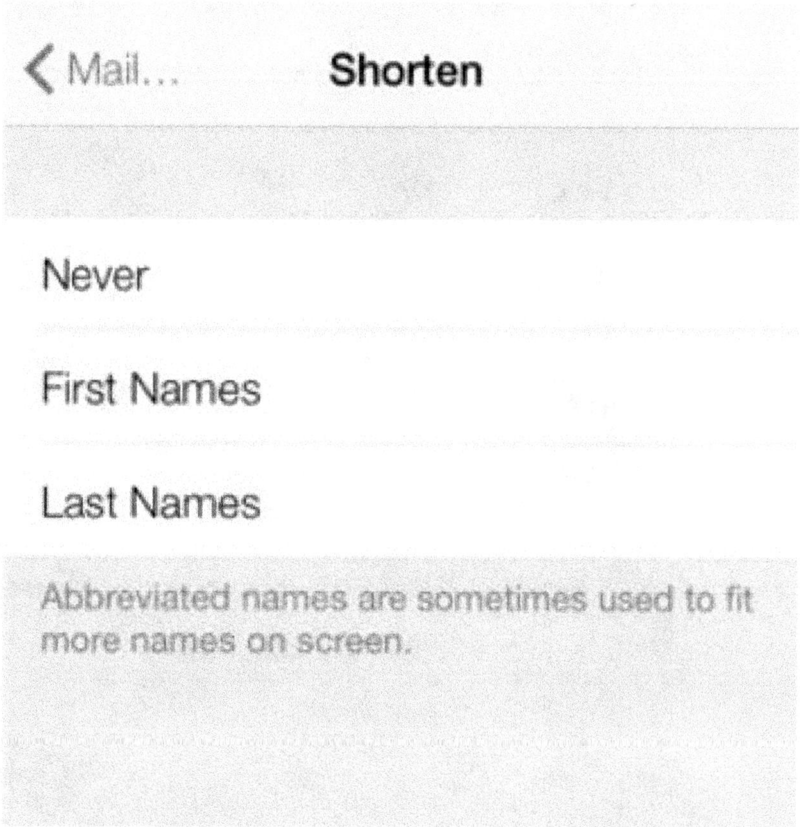

‹ Mail…   **Shorten**

Never

First Names

Last Names

Abbreviated names are sometimes used to fit more names on screen.

Safari's settings as discussed earlier have also been slightly reorganized for your better experience. Private Browsing can now be accessed directly from the Safari app and some settings like Fraud Warning have been renamed to give a more clear description. For example, "Fraudulent Website Warning."

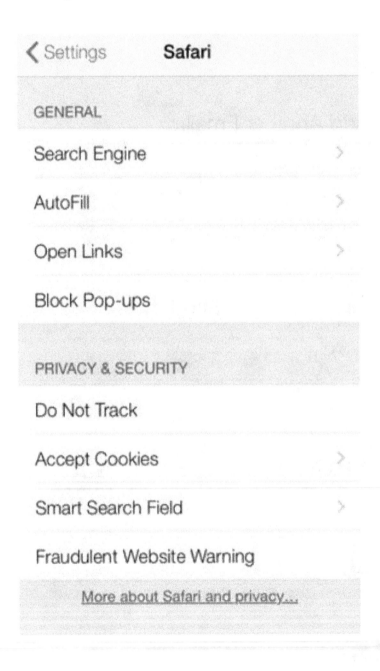

Clear History

Clear Cookies and Data

READING LIST

Use Cellular Data

Use cellular network to save Reading List
items from iCloud for offline reading.

Advanced   >

Cleaner Calculator

C	+/-	%	÷
7	8	9	×
4	5	6	−
1	2	3	+
0	.		=

Apple's good old calculator has been replaced with a sleek, cleaner design calculator. You can also find a comprehensive grid of functions and as well as plain numbers.

(	)	mc	m+	m−	mr
2nd	x^2	x^3	x^y	e^x	10^x
$\frac{1}{x}$	$\sqrt[2]{x}$	$\sqrt[3]{x}$	$\sqrt[x]{y}$	ln	$\log_{10}$
x!	sin	cos	tan	e	EE
Rad	sinh	cosh	tanh	π	Rand

Shortcut to Open Camera App

Now you can access your camera app directly from your lock screen.

Simply tap the camera icon as shown in the figure below.

Find the Right App with App Store

iOS 7's App Store allows you to find out apps that are popular "near you." Well, there's nothing to worry because iOS 7 helps you discover interesting new apps that can make your work easier.

What's Popular Near Me?

Simply tap **Near Me** in App Store and you should see a long list of apps you might find useful.

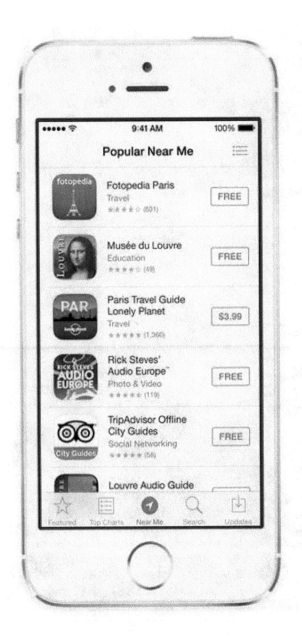

Image Courtesy: www.apple.com

Select the Best Apps for your Kids.

If you just cannot figure out safe apps that can entertain your kids, it is time you ask iOS 7 for help.

All you have to do is visit the App Store and select the Kids category for a comprehensive selection of "age appropriate" apps.

Image Courtesy: www.apple.com

iOS 7 for Business

When it comes to keeping up with the latest business trends, Apple users definitely have an edge. Here are some popular business apps that can help you make the most of your device.

7 Popular iOS 7 Apps for Business

1. Evernote

One of the most popular "note-taking" app has been especially redesigned for iOS 7 users. New features you can see include AirDrop note sharing as well as dynamic sections that only show up when you use them. These sections vanish when not in use. You'll also be impressed with improved image annotations and better, faster data syncing.

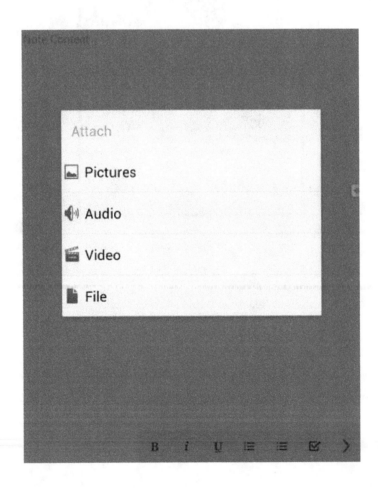

2. Collaborate

This app is a perfect choice if you want to become an efficient project manager and organize group tasks. With Collaborate, you can track task progress, set project deadlines and even share important files via services like Evernote and Google Drive. The iOS 7 version also allows you to send private messages via AirDrop.

Image Courtesy: itunes.apple.com

3. Box Notes

This simple note taking app helps you do extraordinary things. You can note down your thoughts in a simple way and even create notes directly in Box.

It's really easy to attach images, video and rich media files to your notes and share them with your team.

Your team can then brainstorm new ideas, and implement them in the same document, more importantly at the same time. Box Notes pulls every new contact from your list of collaborators.

Image Courtesy: http://content.box.com

4. Skype

The immensely popular video chat app is revamped for iOS 7. The updates allow you to join group calls from your iPhone business contacts and have great video quality chats with family.

iPhone Screenshots

Image Courtesy: itunes.apple.com

5. Fantastical for iPhone

This fast and simple calendar app can schedule meetings for you as well as manage old and new appointments.

iPhone Screenshots

Image Courtesy: itunes.apple.com

6. Google Drive

Like previous versions of iOS, iOS 7 also allows you to edit and share Google docs, spreadsheets and presentations with your friends and team members.

Screenshots

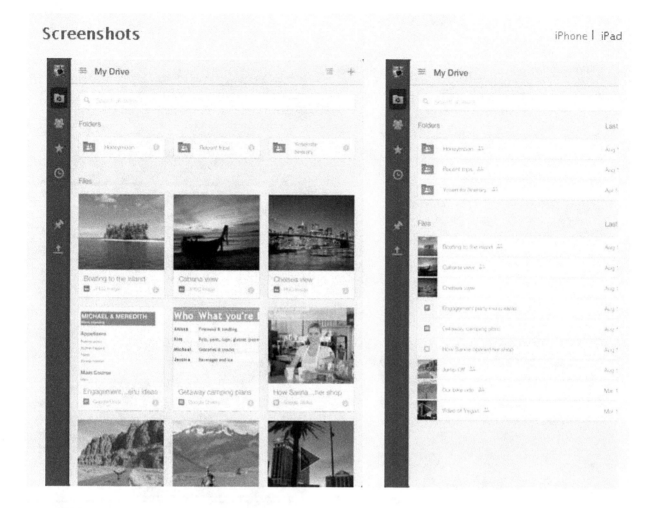

Image Courtesy: itunes.apple.com

7. Mailbox

This exciting email app helps you organize your inbox as a to-do list and it's features have been specially redesigned for iOS 7.

Screenshots

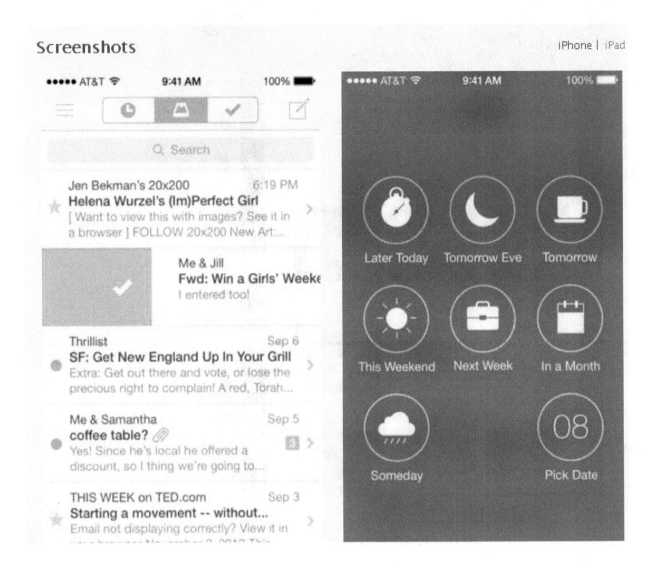

Image Courtesy: itunes.apple.com

The Final Word

Apple has been working diligently on the latest version of its mobile operating system, i.e. iOS 7 and you can see great results. If you haven't yet downloaded the new system, download it today and make your device happy. Here's hoping that you have a great time with your new operating system and it's actually working wonders for you.

www.ingramcontent.com/pod-product-compliance
Lightning Source LLC
Chambersburg PA
CBHW060453060326
40689CB00020B/4511